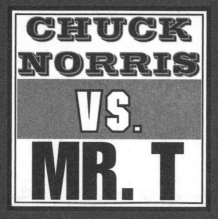

ALSO BY IAN SPECTOR

The Truth About Chuck Norris

400 FACTS ABOUT THE
BADDEST
DUDES
IN THE HISTORY OF EVER

Ian Spector

GOTHAM
BOOKS

GOTHAM BOOKS
Published by Penguin Group (USA) Inc.
375 Hudson Street, New York, New York 10014, U.S.A.
Penguin Group (Canada), 90 Eglinton Avenue East, Suite 700, Toronto, Ontario M4P
2Y3, Canada (a division of Pearson Penguin Canada Inc.); Penguin Books Ltd, 80
Strand, London WC2R 0RL, England; Penguin Ireland, 25 St Stephen's Green, Dublin 2,
Ireland (a division of Penguin Books Ltd); Penguin Group (Australia), 250 Camberwell
Road, Camberwell, Victoria 3124, Australia (a division of Pearson Australia Group
Pty Ltd); Penguin Books India Pvt Ltd, 11 Community Centre, Panchsheel Park, New
Delhi - 110 017, India; Penguin Group (NZ), 67 Apollo Drive, Rosedale, North Shore
0632, New Zealand (a division of Pearson New Zealand Ltd); Penguin Books (South
Africa) (Pty) Ltd, 24 Sturdee Avenue, Rosebank, Johannesburg 2196, South Africa

Penguin Books Ltd, Registered Offices: 80 Strand, London WC2R 0RL, England

Published by Gotham Books, a member of Penguin Group (USA) Inc.

First printing, December 2008

10 9 8 7 6 5

Copyright © 2008 by Ian Spector

Chuck Norris illustrations by Angelo Vildasol. Mr. T illustrations by John Petersen.

All rights reserved

Gotham Books and the skyscraper logo are trademarks of Penguin Group (USA) Inc.

Library of Congress Cataloging-in-Publication Data has been applied for.

ISBN 978-1-592-40465-0

Printed in the United States of America

Set in bad-ass typefaces like ITC MACHINE, Clarendon, Alpin Gothic No. 3, and Monkton
Designed by Sabrina Bowers

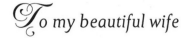 *To my beautiful wife*

and wonderful kids*

---

*I'm not married, and to the best of my knowledge don't
have any kids, but just in case I don't write any books
in the future, I thought I should take advantage of the
opportunity.

INTRODUCTION

A lot has happened since the first book came out. First, and most important, there was a presidential election.

When I started my Web site in April 2005, little did I know that it would have an impact on a presidential election. During the Republican presidential primaries in late 2007, Mike Huckabee was endorsed by none other than Chuck Norris. An advertisement that aired in Iowa during their caucus (which quickly spread across the Internet and became the hit ad of the primary season) featured Mr. Huckabee and Mr. Norris exchanging facts about each other to the viewer. While Chuck pitched his endorsee's views on the second amendment and some such, Huckabee rattled off some genuine Chuck Norris facts. Huckabee went on to win the Iowa caucus, which was viewed by the political establishment as a huge surprise.

I've always believed that these facts are a lot of fun and also, on a basic level, one of the silliest things to ever come out of the Internet. That these facts made it as far as the U.S. presidential race is well, pretty damn astounding. As the whole thing was unfolding, I specifically recall doing an interview for a Canadian radio station, part of which went something like this:

"So, you make this guy famous again, he endorses this candidate in a commercial that becomes famous, and then he wins the Iowa caucus. What happens if he wins the presidency?"

I paused for a bit, taking in the severity of the situation. "That would be quite a turn of events," I replied.

The issue sprawled out into the late-night talk shows as well. There was a public, albeit faux, feud going on between Conan O'Brien and Stephen Colbert about who "made" Mike Huckabee. Conan's view was that his show had for years played random clips from *Walker, Texas Ranger*, which made Chuck Norris famous, who endorsed Huckabee, who made him popular. Colbert refuted that Huckabee won the primary due to multiple appearances on his *Report* and was the recipient of the "Colbert Bump." In an incredible coincidence, I was actually in the audience of *The Colbert Report* when Colbert was making this statement. I had visited the offices of my editor at Gotham earlier that day and had with me a bag full of copies of *The Truth about Chuck Norris* and all I could do was think to myself, *Yeah, right, guys.*

That being said, I don't think—or perhaps I don't want to think—that I was directly involved in Huckabee's short-lived success. If the people in this country will pick their president based on something as absurd as Chuck Norris facts, then we're all a lot worse off than I thought we already were.

The second thing that happened since the publication of the first book: I was sued (by Chuck Norris). It was Friday at about 4 P.M. in December 2007. I was in my local Barnes and Noble looking to buy a copy of my book—mostly because I wanted to give it to a friend, but partially because I like to see employees' reactions when I tell them I wrote it (they are usually less enthused than I expect). As I was navigating to the humor section, I got a call from my editor, Patrick. "We were just served with papers for a lawsuit by Chuck Norris's people," he said. Prior to this there was some correspondence between Mr. Norris's attorneys and myself and Penguin's legal folks. While legal proceedings are inherently serious, I have to admit I cracked a smile after reading in the served papers that one of the reasons we were being sued was that "Mr. Norris is known as an upright citizen to whom God, country, and values are of paramount importance," and that "Mr. Norris also is concerned that the book may conflict with his personal values and thereby tarnish his image and cause him significant personal embarrassment. . . ." This, of course, is despite the fact that he has fathered an illegitimate child according to his autobiography, and that he starred in a number of ultraviolent action movies in the 1980s. I also chuckled when I saw Chuck's real name on the papers: Carlos Ray Norris.

The story was picked up by the newswires over the next few days, and gave us a huge boost in sales. In fact, the book made it to the *New York Times* bestseller list for the first time in early January 2008. The book also reached the following positions on Amazon.com:

- #1 – BOOKS > LITERATURE & FICTION > UNITED STATES
- #1 – BOOKS > LITERATURE & FICTION > WORLD LITERATURE
- #1 – BOOKS > LITERATURE & FICTION > UNITED STATES > HUMOR
- #1 – BOOKS > ENTERTAINMENT > HUMOR > LOVE, SEX & MARRIAGE
- #4 – BOOKS > SPORTS
- #5 – BOOKS > ENTERTAINMENT > HUMOR
- #11 – BOOKS > LITERATURE & FICTION
- #11 – BOOKS > ENTERTAINMENT

I don't know if this says more about consumer habits or Amazon's automated categorization of its inventory, but it was fun to see such great numbers.

Now, without getting into the tedious details of the legal issues, partly because they're *actually* really annoying to recount and read about and partly because neither Mr. Norris, Penguin, nor I can disclose certain information about it, let me just offer the following advice to the reader: Don't get sued. It's a real pain. After months of negotiations, we finally settled in the spring of 2008.

By the way, that Barnes and Noble was out of copies of my book.

Also, since the last book came out, I decided to not do much more of this.

In April 2008, I was asked to speak at a conference about Internet humor called ROFLCon, which was hosted at MIT. I was asked the question, "What are you going to do next?" in front of an audience of several hundred people, which was also being broadcast live on the Internet. I could only answer, "Well, I'm only twenty, and I plan on doing something actually useful with my life." I didn't mean to sound ungrateful to the fans of Chuck Norris facts. I was trying to say (and I think the audience understood) that I'm still really shocked by how big this thing has become, and I've never made life plans around the Chuck Norris phenomenon. But I've got a lot of time ahead of me and have met some incredible people along this crazy journey who I hope to collaborate with in the future.

That's it for now, and I hope you enjoy the new Chuck Norris facts in this edition, as well as the Mr. T facts. A lot of people don't know that I've been collecting Mr. T facts for almost as long as Chuck facts. Maybe Mr. T will get into politics just as Chuck did. At the time of this writing we're not sure who's going to be elected, but let's hope he has the good sense to appoint Mr. T as secretary of defense, director of the department of Homeland Security, and chairman of the National Center for Skull-Crackin'.

A man once told Chuck Norris there was no wrong way to eat a Reese's. Chuck Norris promptly showed him that there was by killing the man's wife with it.

Mr. T's orgasm leaves an exit wound.

Chuck Norris hates Native Americans, even though he's part Native American himself. Chuck Norris also hates irony.

Chuck Norris was the inspiration for Donkey Kong, HD-TV, and waterslides. Yes, waterslides.

In an average living room there are 1,242 objects Mr. T could use to kill you, including the room itself.

Rather than take showers, Chuck Norris rides a nine-foot grizzly bear through a car wash.

Napoleon lost the battle of Waterloo because he couldn't speak English and Mr. T wouldn't lower himself to speaking French.

The famous video footage of Sasquatch is actually Chuck Norris returning to his woodland home.

Statistically speaking, you are more likely to be pitied by Mr. T than you are to have feet.

Chuck Norris stole
your bike.

Chuck Norris doesn't laugh,
he sues.

When Mr. T folds his arms, the U.S. Terrorism Threat Level is raised to Gold.

Hellen Keller's favorite color is Chuck Norris.

Physicists are breathlessly awaiting October 1, 2010. On that day, *The A-Team* will air in high-definition for the first time, and physicists are hoping to glimpse a fundamental particle called the Higgs boson in the eternal blackness of Mr. T's mohawk.

Chuck Norris and Steven Seagal are secretly married. Norris wears the pants.

Mr. T once got into a fight with a ninja. He killed the ninja, but only after the ninja had cut off two of his fingers. Those fingers grew up to be Gary Coleman and Webster.

Chuck Norris feels no attraction to men or women, only to hyperintelligent shades of blue.

After an epic night of drinking, Mr. T took the largest dump ever recorded. What he crapped out ended up being the 1979 Tenth Anniversary Pontiac Trans Am, which he occasionally still drives.

Chuck Norris accidentally created Optimus Prime while trying to come up with a prototype for the Total Gym.

Mr. T has made only one prediction in his life: pain. He was 100 percent accurate.

If you have five dollars and Chuck Norris has five dollars, Chuck Norris has more money than you.

Chuck Norris won't allow his children to be taught evolution at school. This wouldn't be a big deal, but he fathered 70 percent of the people in the southern United States.

Mr. T once said, "There is no I in team, but there is a T! Fool!!" This was at a motivational speaking conference and it was the entirety of his lecture.

The Chinese ideogram for "Chuck Norris" depicts the heaven above, growing a beard.

Mr. T was present at the wedding in Cana when Jesus turned water into wine. Not to be outdone, Mr. T took Jesus's wine and turned it into funk.

God once made a rock so big that not even he could lift it, thus answering the legendary philosophical question. Chuck Norris not only lifted this rock, but also karate chopped it so hard that it fragmented and formed the progressive rock group Yes.

Mr. T once punched Jesus in the face just to prove that he could.

A freak accident involving Chuck Norris and a severe thunderstorm turned an ordinary Total Gym into Richard Dean Anderson, star of TV series *MacGyver*. Scholars around the world maintain that this is the only known case of irony that is both situational and dramatic.

Don't think for even a second that Mr. T didn't invent T-bagging, because he'd be more than happy to demonstrate it for you.

Chuck Norris can play the bongo drums with his hands behind his back. He accomplishes this by leaning over them really close and flexing his pecs. The sweet rhythms he produces are the most potent form of aphrodisiac known to man.

In the director's cut of *Rocky III*, Mr. T not only defeats Rocky . . . he tears his arm off and beats Adrian to death with it.

Chuck Norris coined the phrase "I could eat a horse" after he ate the last unicorn in existence.

Mr. T will sometimes tease Jesus because it took him three whole days to rise from the dead.

Many people say that Chuck Norris eats babies. This is not true. Babies just want to be in Chuck Norris's stomach.

The first alphabet consisted of only the letters M, R, and T. Other letters eventually had to be created in order to describe things that were not, in fact, awesome.

In 1979, Chuck Norris became the first black man to win the New York City Marathon.

Mr. T's autobiography, *So Many Fools, Not Enough Pity,* was awarded the Pulitzer Prize for its heart-warming and inspiring tales of Mr. T overcoming his fear of flying and his battle with gold addiction—as well as the sweet tutorial on how to install machine-gun turrets on top of a GMC van using a welding torch, a fifty-five-gallon drum, chicken wire, and skim milk.

When Mr. T goes to kick a field goal, he has to aim for goalposts in a different stadium, just to make it fair.

Chuck Norris ate the last piece of pizza.

What are you gonna do about it?

A random onlooker once taunted Mr. T.
Mr. T responded by hitting the man so hard that both his parents died.

If you disagree with Chuck Norris, he'll karate chop you into a bajillion pieces. He is aware that this is not a number, but if you call him on it, he'll round-house kick you into a quabillion.

Mr. T once punched a double-decker bus so hard that it crapped out a Mini Cooper.

Chuck Norris can beat a brick wall in tennis.

God didn't create the world, he only drew the blueprints. Mr. T built the world with his bare hands, an acetylene torch, and a fifty-five-gallon drum.

Chuck Norris drives an ice-cream truck covered in human skulls.

According to Mr. T, Jibba Jabba is the official language of 99.9 percent of the world's population.

Chuck Norris represents the East Side, but

has the West Coast rappers under his control, too.

Mr. T was once the judge at an interpretive dance competition. He found them guilty.

A midget, a rabbi, and a horse all walk into a bar. Ah, fuck it. Chuck Norris roundhouse kicked all their asses.

When Mr. T was being knighted, the Queen knelt for him.

Chuck Norris was the original model for Brawny paper towels. He gained this position by winning a competition to see who could best intimidate a woman into a life of cleaning and servitude.

The only reason *The A-Team* was canceled was that it cost more than $2 million an episode in special effects to create the illusion that it had taken Mr. T a whole twenty-six minutes to defeat some bad guys.

If you watch *Walker, Texas Ranger* closely, you'll notice that Chuck Norris uses violence only as a last resort, or when the world goes in slow motion.

Mr. T's full name is Dr. Mr. T because he has a Ph.D. in Being the Greatest Man Alive.

Chuck Norris has secretly kept a speech for an Oscar® win for the last twenty-five years. It starts, "I can't fucking believe this either, but . . . "

At his current pace, Mr. T will have pitied every man, woman, and child ever born by the year 2012. At that point, he will ascend to heaven to take his rightful place as God's bouncer.

Chuck Norris rescued thirteen infants from Charity Hospital following the devastation of Hurricane Katrina. He did not have a boat. He has not returned the babies.

Mr. T's umbilical cord was actually a large gold chain. The medallion didn't grow in until he was six months old.

If you paint one painting, you're not a painter. But Chuck Norris baked one cake, and he currently holds the title of World's Best Baker.

When he heard that Sylvester Stallone was planning to make *Rocky VI,* Mr. T said, "This time I really do pity the fool."

Chuck Norris is a man's man's man.

The only thing blacker than Mr. T's skin is
his heart.

Chuck Norris eats beef jerky and shits gunpowder. Then he uses that gunpowder to make a bullet, which he uses to kill a cow and make more beef jerky. Some people refer to this as the "Circle of Life."

Mr. T has both the right to bear arms and the right to bare arms.

Chuck Norris made killing cool. Before everybody was, like, "Killing? Yeah, right!" But now everybody is, like, "Sweet."

Mr. T can count to ten left-handed.

Chuck Norris's sperm are approximately the size of red salmon. When Chuck's sperm mature, they travel up a river to be caught and eaten by thirsty Japanese girls.

Special relativity applies in two cases: when you pass the event horizon of a black hole, and while walking within thirty feet of Mr. T.

Sometimes Mr. T gets up in the middle of the night and lifts weights in his sleep.

Chuck Norris has no pancreas. He instead has a retroperitoneal waffle iron that excretes a pancreatic juice made of liquid vengeance.

Mr. T is allergic to doorknobs. That's why he can only kick through doors.

Chuck Norris got in touch with his feminine side, and promptly got her pregnant.

Mr. T once gave the Smurfs a beatdown so bad they were forced to relocate underwater and become the Snorks.

Chuck Norris was actually Dr. Martin Luther King, Jr.'s dream.

Mr. T has won every game of Yahtzee and Bingo, but has never uttered either word.

In the game of life, Chuck Norris has the only retired jersey.

Mr. T's diet consists entirely of Spam and washed-up child actors. He actually recieved a court order to remove Macaulay Culkin from his lower intestine so he could testify at the Michael Jackson trial.

Chuck Norris is just like Jesus, except Chuck Norris won't die for your sins. Instead, you'll die for his.

Mr. T stays in shape by doing one hundred pull-ups a day. **With his wiener.**

Chuck Norris once decided to make a vibrator that would simulate the size and power of his actual penis. The result was a baseball bat wrapped in barbed wire and bolted to a jackhammer.

Mr. T has the ability to lactate, and will sometimes allow orphans to nurse at his bosom. However, his breast milk has such a high concentration of calcium that it instantly fossilizes any infant who drinks it.

Chuck Norris often asks people to pull his finger. When they do, he round-houses them in the abdomen. Then he farts.

When Mr. T accepted the Academy Award® for Best Supporting Actor for his role in *Rocky III*, he thanked Chuck Norris for blazing a path for actors persecuted due to their lack of acting ability.

Bruce Lee never died. The true cause of his disappearance is that he asked Chuck Norris to teach him how to perform a roundhouse kick. Being good friends, Chuck Norris promised to teach him, but only after Bruce Lee embarked on an epic journey of the spirit that is still taking place entirely within Chuck Norris's beard.

King Kong once challenged Godzilla to an arm-wrestling match. Mr. T won.

Chuck Norris keeps trying to donate sperm, but the receptionist keeps getting pregnant.

Mr. T was supposed to be on the American dollar bill, but the bill would become so valuable that no one but Mr. T could afford it.

Chuck Norris saved President Bush from choking on a pretzel by round-house kicking him in the throat. Chuck had no idea he was choking.

Chuck Norris does not open doors for his date. He roundhouse kicks them down. Her, too.

If at the exact same moment, the same person was pitied by Mr. T and roundhouse kicked by Chuck Norris, **the universe would implode.**

There is nothing to fear but fear itself, and fear itself fears Chuck Norris.

The toy surprise in boxes of Mr. T cereal consisted of an actual gold chain. Mr. T was good at busting heads, but never was much of a businessman.

Chuck Norris once roundhouse kicked a waitress because his steak didn't have a beard.

Chuck Norris uses ribbed condoms inside out, so he gets the pleasure.

There is not and never will be a Mrs. T.

Chuck Norris is so good he'll shit your pants for you.

The last time Mr. T uttered the words "I pity the fool," a man in Colorado suddenly died for no reason.

Chuck Norris does not have AIDS but he gives it to people anyway.

Mr. T pisses molten steel.

If you look in a mirror and say "Chuck Norris" three times, he will appear and kill your entire family . . . but at least you get to see Chuck Norris.

The inventor of TiVo was inspired by a divine vision sent by God, who couldn't decide what to watch when *The A-Team* and *Walker, Texas Ranger* once aired at the same time.

Chuck Norris has won every contest that he's entered. Even Miss Nude Wisconsin.

Mr. T's edition of the VH1 show *Where Are They Now?* was the shortest in the show's history. It was ten seconds long and consisted of a black screen with the words "Right Behind You" written on it.

Rather than drink a cup of coffee every morning, Chuck Norris pours the whole pot on his genitals.

$$E = Mr. T^2$$

Chuck Norris eats three square meals a day. His beard eats seven.

Sometimes, it is said, when you hold a gold chain to your ear you can hear the screams of all the fools Mr. T has beaten to death.

When Chuck Norris roundhouse kicks you, he tears a hole in the fabric of space and time, which sucks you into a parallel universe filled with Chuck Norrises, all waiting to roundhouse kick you.

Mr. T actually coined the phrase "I pity the fool!" during a philosophical debate with Kierkegaard in Copenhagen in 1848.

In the 2008 Summer Olympics, Michael Phelps won eight gold medals. Shortly thereafter, Mr. T won eight gold medals in the parking lot of the Beijing National Aquatics Center. Mr. T is still trying to get Scaring the Shit Out of Michael Phelps recognized as an official Olympic event.

Chuck Norris doesn't need a weapon.

He is one.

The American flag puts its hand over its heart anytime Mr. T walks by.

Whenever Chuck Norris sees a Best Buy, he burns it to the ground, because he firmly believes that a Total Gym for three easy payments of $19.99 is the best buy you'll ever find.

When Mr. T goes black, he can come back.

Chuck Norris used the majority of the money he made for *Missing in Action 2* to have the inside of his wife's vagina lined with denim.

The creators of the original Mortal Kombat video game got the idea for "fatality" finishing moves after watching Mr. T conduct a course on international diplomacy at Harvard.

Chuck Norris has had sex on every Total Gym that has been sold in the Midwest.

Mr. T invented mathematics to record how many fools he's pitied.

Chuck Norris's first girlfriend gave him the nickname "7-11" because he was 7 inches limp and 11 hard. They broke up when he was 8.

Mr. T's birthday is every day. It took God 365 days to create him.

Chuck Norris was to appear in the Street Fighter II video game, but was removed by programmers because every button caused him to do a roundhouse kick. When asked about this "glitch," Norris replied, **"That's no glitch."**

There is an eleventh commandment, edited out of the Bible, that says, "None of the above applies to Mr. T."

Chuck Norris can mathematically make two wrongs equal a right.

"Casual Fridays" were started so that businessmen could work at least one day a week without fear of Mr. T strangling them with their own ties.

Chuck Norris eats dinosaur bones and craps out high-grade petroleum.

Mr. T once swallowed Corey Feldman and pooped out Corey Haim.

Chuck Norris ate mathematician Pierre de Fermat and crapped out a proof to his Last Theorem. (Chuck's colon is Lucasian Professor of Mathematics at Cambridge University.)

Whenever Chuck Norris successfully completes a vicious roundhouse kick to the face he sings to himself "This Is How We Do It" by Montel Jordan.

Mr. T's mohawk is maintained by a community of Buddhist monks living on his scalp.

When *Walker, Texas Ranger* aired for the first time in high definition, 300,000 women in the Midwest had simultaneous orgasms.

Everyone has a skeleton in their closet.

Chuck Norris has 7,483.

On the seventh day, God created Mr. T. Then they both chilled out and watched the game.

The term *nunchuck* was coined after Chuck Norris used a pair of Catholic nuns as weapons to mercilessly beat an angry mob to death. Chuck makes weapons from his surroundings.

Mr. T is an asshole. By saying that, my life expectancy is now three seco

Every wall in Chuck Norris's house is a mirror because Chuck Norris must always be surrounded by beauty.

Mr. T pities Asia. The continent *and* the band.

Jesus's birthday isn't December 25th, but Chuck Norris once sent him a birthday card on that day. Jesus was too scared to tell Chuck the truth, and that's why we celebrate Christmas.

Mr. T loves children, because they're just small enough to be forgiven for any foolish behavior but just large enough that Mr. T doesn't get the temptation to swallow them.

Chuck Norris banged Christie Brinkley, and nine months later she gave birth to the Total Gym.

If you were ever foolish enough to get into a fight with Mr. T, there would be only two hits: Mr. T hitting you, and you hitting the surface of the sun.

Scientists have attempted to calculate the statistical possibilty of anyone beating Chuck Norris. The sheer impossibility of this task has caused many of the scientists to develop severe foot-shaped bruising to the face.

Mr. T doesn't step on toes.
Mr. T steps on necks.

It is said you can't know someone until you walk a mile in their shoes. This means no one will ever know Chuck Norris because he'd kill you if you touched his shoes.

Mr. T can mix iced tea so strong, it allows you to see through time.

Chuck Norris will eat your soul for a Klondike Bar.

In the event that the president, vice president, speaker of the house, president pro tempore, and the cabinet all die, Mr. T becomes our theocratic leader.

In five hundred years, pure energy will be observable under a very sophisticated microscope. When viewed, you will be able to see millions of Chuck Norrises doing roundhouse kicks nonstop at an incredible rate. When this happens, Chuck will emerge from his grave after a long sleep, stretch his arms, and casually say, "I cannot be created or destroyed."

Mr. T sleeps with a pillow under his gun.

Chuck Norris does not obey the Law of Conservation of Energy, choosing instead to obey the Law of Distribution of Pain.

When Mr. T gets hot or nervous, he starts sweating bullets. Fifty-caliber hollow-point bullets.

Chuck Norris masturbates to pictures of himself masturbating.

Mr. T is the original Black Power Ranger.

After hearing that Jesus had fed multitudes with five loaves of bread and two fish, Chuck Norris fed the entire population of India with just the crumbs in his mustache.

If you look right into Mr. T's eyes for more than quick two-second bursts, you will crap out your internal organs in alphabetical order.

Chuck Norris's sperm is so virile that it traveled back in time and impregnated his mother. Only Chuck Norris could father Chuck Norris.

Mr. T discovered America. He called the natives Indians not because he thought he was in India, but because he thought it was funny. Which it was.

If you put a picture of Chuck Norris on a record and play it backward, you'll hear the *Walker, Texas Ranger* theme song followed by a raspy voice that says, "Seven days." Seven days later, Chuck Norris will explode into your home and raid your refrigerator.

Chuck Norris enjoys ruining the endings of Harry Potter books for children. When they start crying, Chuck Norris calmly says, "I'll give you something to cry about," and roundhouse kicks them in the face.

When Mr. T sleeps, he stores his gold chains in a special closet built for this purpose. We know this place as Fort Knox.

Chuck Norris can make Communism work, but he never would.

Mr. T was the original host of *Pimp My Ride*. He was fired halfway through the first season after installing machine gun turrets and gold-chain steering wheels on every vehicle.

On a hot Texas day, Chuck Norris heard someone say, "It's not the heat, it's the humidity that will kill you." Chuck immediately threw him into the sun.

At *WrestleMania 2*, Mr. T sneezed backstage. Hulk Hogan has been bald ever since.

Chuck Norris is no longer a noun;
it is a verb.

Mr. T can punch you and pity you three times
before you hit the ground.

Chuck Norris once had sex on the
beach. The lucky woman exploded
from the sheer force of his ejaculation.
However, his sperm lived on and occasionally wash up on shore, where they
are mistakenly identified as giant squid.

Mr. T took over the part of Captain Kirk on *Star Trek* for three seasons, but is such a talented actor that no one noticed.

Chuck Norris doesn't get morning wood, he gets morning redwood.

Twenty-three. That's the number of people Mr. T has pitied in the time it has taken you to read this sentence.

At this very moment, there is a fifty-fifty chance that **Chuck Norris** is boning your sister.

Chuck Norris is the reason why you touch yourself at night.

George Washington threw a silver dollar across the Potomac River. Mr. T did the same thing . . .

from Denver.

Chuck Norris has never used a question mark in his entire life.

The theme song to *Law & Order* is the exact sound of Mr. T's heartbeat.

The only word in the English language that rhymes with orange is Chuck Norris.

If Dracula survives off human blood, guess who survives off Dracula's blood? Yup, Mr. T.

Chuck Norris uses his penis to look around corners.

What you see, Mr. T sees. What you don't see? Don't worry, Mr. T sees that, too.

Chuck Norris doesn't bathe like the rest of us. The only baths Chuck Norris takes are bloodbaths.

Mr. T holds the copyright on the letter T. Every time the letter appears in print, Mr. T receives a check in the mail for $13.50.

Chuck Norris doesn't know the meaning of wartime—all he knows is game time.

Mr. T invented Thomas Edison.

When people are dying, they are told not to go to the light, because Chuck Norris is there waiting to kill them.

While filming *Rocky III*, Mr. T punched Sylvester Stallone so hard Sly spoke clearly for a week.

Chuck Norris knows Victoria's secret.

Mr. T invented the X-ray, the G-string, the R-rating, and Jay-Z after a drunken bender caused him to momentarily forget which letter he was.

Bigfoot is a piece of Chuck Norris's beard that gained sentience and escaped.

When Dr. Bruce Banner gets angry, he turns into the Hulk. When the Hulk gets angry, he turns into Mr. T.

Mr. T concluded the Civil Rights movement by getting on a bus one time. All the white people immediately moved to the back.

Chuck Norris doesn't wait for opportunity to come knocking. He roundhouse kicks it till he gets what he wants.

Mr. T pities fools at such a high frequency that only dogs can hear it.

In response to his challenge, Chuck Norris roundhouse kicked MC Hammer so hard that he went bankrupt. Chuck Norris then bellowed, "I can touch this," while he thrusted his pelvis in Hammer's direction.

Mr. T was fired from the Psychic Friends Network for always predicting pain.

To Chuck Norris, doorknobs and toilets are seen as merely suggestions.

Chuck Norris circumcised himself.
At birth. With his bare hands.

Mr. T's middle name is actually "period."

Chuck Norris CAN find a needle in a
haystack, and then kill a man with the
needle . . . or the haystack.

Mr. T's incredible greatness has been attributed to the fact that his genetic code doesn't have any A, G, or C. His genetic code is in fact, nothing but Ts.

Chuck Norris constructed his own iPod by staring intensely at ten thousand country-western bands until they fearfully compacted themselves into a 2 x 4 x ½-inch white rectangle.

Don't ever call Mr. T just T. Someone did, just once.

Chuck Norris is so cool that the Pope has a fish decal on his car with the word *Norris* inside.

Mr. T does not play the guitar, but he will bash your face in with one.

Chuck Norris's shoes, most notably the one that roundhouse kicked down the Berlin Wall, are kept in a secret government closet in Langley, Virginia.

All those diamonds in Mr. T's jewelry? They were a bag of charcoal this morning.

Chuck Norris never wet his bed as a child. The bed wet itself out of fear.

Mr. T invented fools. Realizing the magnitude of his folly, he then created pity.

Chuck Norris tells time by staring directly into the sun.

Mr. T's mohawk makes him more aerodynamically engineered to pity you.

Chuck Norris went into a kindergarten to talk about fire safety. After four minutes, three children were on fire and Chuck had shot a bottle-rocket out of his urethra.

When Chuck Norris visited the Vatican, he took the Pope's confession.

Mr. T went through 257 Sylvester Stallone stunt doubles during the taping of *Rocky III*.

Chuck Norris was cast as the protagonist in *Terminator*, but he later bowed out of the role, since he has already stopped a time war between machines and mankind. Twice.

Each tablet of Viagra contains one drop of Mr. T's sweat.

Every morning Mr. T shaves off the previous day's mohawk and sends it to NASA to use as shuttle re-entry heat-shield tiles.

Chuck Norris performs cold fusion in his left testicle, and nuclear fission in his right.

Mr. T's mom didn't like his haircut. So he punched her in the mouth.

Mr. T wears bear traps for sandals.

Chuck Norris: Impregnating virgins,
and keeping them that way, since
9 months B.C.

Mr. T eats cancer for breakfast.

Chuck Norris actually sang the *Walker, Texas Ranger* theme song. This is not a joke. He actually fucking sang it.

You don't want to know what Mr. T did to Misters A through S.

For every man you don't kill, Chuck Norris kills seven.

Mr. T is the only thing keeping the rainforests from killing us.

Chuck Norris can deep-throat a wiffleball bat.

Mr. T's pity for fools is used by mathematicians as a demonstration of the concept of infinity.

Chuck Norris can grant wishes, as long as you wish for roundhouse kicks to the face or a Total Gym.

The film *Brokeback Mountain* was originally cast with Mr. T and Chuck Norris. The sole reason the two legends declined the starring roles is because if Mr. T and Chuck Norris were to kiss, God would die.

Every four years, Chuck Norris
beats another twenty-four hours into
February.

Mr. T is not black. It's just that the sun is afraid to
shine on him.

When an airport worker told Chuck
Norris that his flight was delayed, he
told her that her pregnancy was delayed
and did jumping jacks on her uterus.

There are only four horsemen of the apocalypse because Mr. T is going to walk.

Mr. T singlehandedly canceled *Friends* by frowning one time.

God wanted ten days to create the world. Chuck Norris gave him six.

Mr. T speaks only when necessary. His main form of communication is folding his arms and slowly shaking his head. And regardless of the situation, he is always understood.

Debbie did Dallas because she couldn't handle Chuck Norris.

The television show *Lost* is loosely based on an inner ear infection Mr. T had as a child.

If Chuck Norris was an animal, he would be a Chuck Norris.

Behind every great man, there is a great woman. Plowing that woman is Mr. T.

Chuck Norris burned his eyeballs out with cigarettes just to prove to some eighth-grade students that smoking is dangerous.

Ask not for whom Mr. T pities; he pities thee.

Chuck Norris's favorite smell is that of his opponent's soiled pants.

Tupac wouldn't be dead if he hadn't eaten Mr. T's Cheetos.

If you want to wear the same cologne as Chuck Norris, you'll be disappointed to find that Chuck Norris doesn't wear cologne. For two hundred dollars, however, Mr. Norris will fart on your chest before you go on a date.

Mr. T once saved *Sesame Street* from bankrupcy by
suggesting they be sponsored by letters . . .
such as T.

God wonders if Chuck Norris is human,
because he sure as hell never created
him.

Mr. T has only one letter in his name because before
his mom could say "Terrell," he strangled her with
the umbilical cord.

There was a time when Mr. T didn't pity fools. That time was called **NEVER**.

The great Chicago fire of 1871 was not, in fact, started by Mrs. O'Leary's cow. The fire was started by Chuck Norris when he discovered that deep-dish pizza had not yet been invented.

Mr. T never learned to read. Letters learned to accommodate Mr. T's mind.

Mr. T and Chuck Norris teamed up in 1989 to bring down the Soviet Union. Their amazing story of struggle, hope, and redemption was adapted for the silver screen as *White Men Can't Jump*.

Chuck Norris has two speeds: "kill" and "fuck your girlfriend."

Mr. T's real last name is Tureaud, but
it's pronounced "Deathblow," fool.

Two and a Half Men was originally a show only about Chuck Norris.

When God said, "Let there be light?" he was asking
Mr. T.

If international politics were a nail,
Chuck Norris would be the hammer. If
international politics were a chance for
all men to embrace each other and live
in peace, Chuck Norris would be the
hammer.

That's not even a T. It's a stick figure drawing of
you, decapitated and legless.

If MacGyver and Chuck were locked in a room together, Chuck would make a bomb out of MacGyver and get out.

Mr. T coined the phrase "Pardon my French" after picking up a Frenchman and using him like a bat to club people.

Chuck Norris is the founder of all modern psychoanalysis.

The Mohawk Indians and the
Mr. T fan club are one and
the same.

Not only does Chuck Norris talk in
the third person, he sees in the third
person.

When Mr. T gets mad, there is no mad left for anyone else.

Chuck Norris takes no prisoners, but he does take their wives.

The movie *Shaft* was Mr. T's penis's biopic.

Life is like a box of chocolates. You never know when Chuck Norris is going to kill you.

Mr. T never blinks. . . . If he did, the entire universe would cease to exist.

Looking for a safe stance on abortion? Neither is Chuck Norris.

Mr. T is Voltron's personal trainer.

Mr. T's penis has a mohawk.

Chuck Norris successfully mated a graham cracker with a knife.

Mr. T doesn't need to believe in God. God believes in Him.

Mr. T's mohawk and Chuck Norris's beard mated. The result was King Kong.

On Chuck Norris's doghouse there is a sticker that says BEWARE OF CHUCK NORRIS.

Mr. T's sweat is both the cause and cure for AIDS.

Chuck Norris is a lot like fine wine: he only gets better with age; and if you hang around with him long enough, you'll probably wake up in a daze, with no money and a bootmark imprinted in your skull.

Mr. T is what Willis was talkin' about.

Chuck Norris played the tornado in the movie *Twister*.

Seismology is the study of Chuck Norris's masturbation habits.

Mr. T's adrenaline is secreted through his biceps in the form of hand grenades.

When you ask Chuck Norris for an autograph, he burns his name onto your soul with his eye lasers.

The original symbol for gold on the periodic table was T.

Chuck Norris doesn't lie. He bends the truth with his massive biceps.

In 1989, Mr. T systematically abducted, tortured, and killed every member of the band Mr. Mister for stealing his first name.

Chuck Norris does not recognize Albany as the capital of New York.

Mr. T was not born, he was discovered.

If at first you don't succeed, **you are obviously not Chuck Norris.**

One day an Indian came and told Mr. T he had a nice mohawk. Mr. T then took his land and made casinos.

Matthew Webb was the first person to swim the English Channel. Chuck Norris was the first person to swim the Sea of Tranquility.

When Mr. T was circumcised, his foreskin was not disposed of. Instead it was raised as a normal child, and it grew to love the game of basketball. Today we know Mr. T's foreskin as Shaquille O'Neal.

Chuck Norris roundhouse kicked his grandmother in the mouth on Christmas morning. Socks again.

The phrase MADE BY CHUCK NORRIS is imprinted beneath the surface of China.

Each of the links on each of Mr. T's gold chains is actually made up of smaller Mr. Ts. Each of those Mr. Ts wears gold chains that are also made up of much smaller Mr. Ts. Our universe exists in the imagination of a Mr. T that is part of thirty-eight greater gold chains.

When Chuck Norris talks about "pumping iron," he's actually referring to masturbation.

Chuck Norris has 189 STDs, including six found only in sharks.

On the day Mr. T dies, there will be one thousand days of mourning. During which time a cold rain will fall constantly, no bird shall sing, and all children will be born hooved and antlered.

Every time Chuck Norris kills someone, an angel gets its beard.

And every time Mr. T pities a fool, an angel gets its mohawk.

Chuck Norris is allowed to talk about Fight Club.

Mr. T doesn't feel pain; pain feels Mr. T.

The term TGIF was coined when statisticians found that Friday is the day with the lowest number of deaths caused by Chuck Norris.

Mr. T is not to scale. His earrings are actually hula hoops.

When God sneezes, the seraphim sing, "Chuck bless you."

Since the presence of Chuck Norris drives women wild with desire and makes men quake with terror, it is very disruptive to film him with other actors. For each episode of *Walker, Texas Ranger*, Chuck Norris filmed his scenes in front of a blue screen and the other actors were digitally added later. This is why his acting appears, occasionally, to be a little wooden.

It took five women ten years to give birth to Mr. T.

A full-scale replica of Chuck Norris's penis was erected in Toronto. It was named the CN Tower in his honor.

Mr. T's hair is not a statement, it's the map to eternal ass whooping.

Chuck Norris allows churches to exist only in order to stop people from coming and praying at his house.

Mr. T coined the phrase "I see dead people" after the waitstaff at Denny's forgot his birthday.

Chuck Norris once survived a suicide bombing. He was the bomber.

Mr. T's pants are made from 100 percent real Godzilla skin.

On orders from Chuck Norris, Crayola created a Chuck Norris–colored crayon. No matter what you try to draw, a picture of Chuck giving you a thumbs-up appears.

Taxes are just the government's way of reimbursing Mr. T for single-handedly winning World War II.

Mr. T is the only man ever to have literally beaten the odds.

Chuck Norris has to sort his laundry into three loads: darks, whites, and bloodstains.

New archeological evidence suggests that it was Mr. T who defeated the giant Goliath. It also suggests that the tiny pebble was actually David.

An average adult's intestines produce about half a liter of flatulent gas per day. Chuck Norris's intestines produce four feature-length films every year, all written and directed by his spleen.

When Mr. T's daughter lost her virginity, Mr. T went out and got it back.

Chuck Norris can pause live TV without using TiVo. He just tells it to hold still while he gets his roast beef sandwich.

Mr. T has directed only one movie in his career. That movie was *You've Got Mail* and it won thirteen Academy Awards®.

The McRib sandwich comes back only when Chuck Norris is in the mood for one.

When installing a video player in his GMC van in 1983, Mr. T went with VHS over Betamax. The rest, as they say, is history.

When Chuck Norris helps you jump-start your car, remember: beard is positive, fist is negative.

If Mr. T and The Fonz were ever to high-five, it would bring about another Ice Age.

Chuck Norris was disqualified from the 1992 Olympic shot-put championship for **reversing the polarity of Earth.**

Mr. T made hate crimes funny again.

While everyone made paper airplanes as a child, Chuck Norris made paper beards.

During the last Ice Age, Mr. T and Chuck Norris encountered each other on a lonesome path in the Alps. Before the inevitable battle could begin, the earth shit itself and created France.

The Chuck Norris action figure is responsible for 84 percent of all cases of Sudden Infant Death Syndrome.

The top three causes of death in this country are heart disease, cancer, and Mr. T ripping out your soul.

A man once spent three days climbing a mountain only to discover that he was scaling Chuck Norris's penis.

The devil sold his soul to spend **one minute as Mr. T.**

Chuck Norris can impregnate a woman in forty-seven ways not involving his penis.

Little known fact: Mr. T's mohawk and Chuck Norris's beard are actually second cousins.

On the series finale of *Fear Factor*, Chuck Norris ate Joe Rogan.

Before Chuck Norris was born, people cried only out of happiness.

Mr. T is one part gold, two parts muscle, one part anger, and **no parts jibba jabba.**

Chuck Norris once spent a night in a hotel in West Virginia. The next day the state promptly changed its name to West Ia.

Scientists theorize that Mr. T cannot catch AIDS because his T-cells pity the virus into submission. The study of this phenomenon would lead to an AIDS vaccine; however, doctors cannot obtain a blood sample because science has been unable to invent a hypodermic needle capable of piercing Mr. T's skin.

Chuck Norris won a car on *The Price Is Right* by guessing that a can of tuna was worth $9,534.

At a press conference following the release of *Rocky III*, a reporter asked Mr. T if he was ever going to change his hairstyle from a mohawk to a more contemporary style. There were no survivors.

Chuck Norris and the Dalai Lama combined to become the perfect human being and the Dalai Lama.

When Mr. T pours his Alpha Bits cereal into a bowl, only Ts come out.

Chuck Norris owns a magical mirror that allows him to peer out of any other mirror in the world. Anytime you undress in front of the mirror in your bedroom, Chuck Norris could be watching. But he never is, because your flabby body disgusts him.

Dick Cheney asked Mr. T to help in the war on terror, but Mr. T only creates terror.

The book *How to Eat Fried Worms* was a highly edited version of Chuck Norris's original *How to Decapitate Foreign Delegations*.

Chuck Norris can peel potatoes with his eyelids.

Most people don't know that Mr. T is actually the Last of the Mohicans. He just doesn't play that card because he wants it to be fair when he applies to law school.

Chuck Norris will make you an offer you can't refuse, and then make you refuse it.

Mr. T doesn't breathe. He holds air hostage.

Chuck Norris's weakness is that he can't kick ass without eating breakfast. Ironically, he eats ass for breakfast.

There is no Control key on Mr. T's keyboard. Mr. T is always in control.

The reason newborn babies cry is because they know they have just entered a world with Chuck Norris.

Complaining of back pain, Atlas once asked Mr. T to hold up the world for him. Mr. T agreed, on the condition that in exchange, Atlas would wear Mr. T's golden necklaces. After five minutes of excruciating pain, Atlas asked for the world back.

God recently converted to Chucktianity.

Mr. T is the reason your kid is black.

If you spell Chuck Norris wrong on Google it doesn't say, "Did you mean: Chuck Norris?" It simply replies, "Run while you still have the chance."

Chuck Norris never retreats. He just attacks in the opposite direction.

Mr. T can keep both feet on the ground and kick ass at the same time.

Jesus can walk on water, but Chuck Norris can swim through land.

Mr. T sleeps once every two weeks for half an hour, standing up, with his eyes open, and he looks pissed off the whole time.

Chuck Norris can kill two stones with one bird.

Mr. T can strangle you with a cordless phone.

If you play Led Zeppelin's "Stairway to Heaven" backward, you'll hear Chuck Norris banging your sister.

Chuck Norris can play the violin with a piano.

Mr. T once made a paraplegic run for his life.

Chuck Norris defeated the Cyclops by punching him between the eye.

Chuck Norris consults a physician when he has an erection lasting less than four hours.

The last man to make eye contact with Mr. T was Stevie Wonder.

Chuck Norris puts the **rage** in **courage**.

When Chuck Norris was born, the nurse said, "Holy crap! That's Chuck Norris!" Then she had had sex with him. At that point, she was the third woman he had slept with.

Mr. T can beat a man to death with his own corpse.

A waitress at a Sizzler accidentally gave Chuck Norris a well-done steak instead of a rare steak. Chuck proceeded to have sex with her on the table and said "Now that's well done!" The waitress replied, "That's pretty rare, too!" Chuck then had sex with her fifteen more times just to prove her wrong.

Vanessa Carlton's hit song "A Thousand Miles" was inspired by the distance Chuck Norris kicked her boyfriend after he stepped on Chuck's snakeskin boots.

Teenage Mutant Ninja Turtles is based on a true story: Chuck Norris once swallowed a turtle whole, and when he crapped it out the turtle was six feet tall and had learned karate.

Mr. T hates golf so much that he smacked half the black out of Tiger Woods.

When you're Chuck Norris, anything plus anything is equal to one. One roundhouse kick to the face.

Chuck Norris never goes to the dentist, because his teeth are unbreakable. His enemies never go to the dentist, because they have no teeth.

Mr. T once beat Usain Bolt in the hundred-meter dash. Mr. T didn't even know he was racing; someone near the finish line had just leaned against his Toyota Camry.

Chuck Norris once pulled out a single hair from his beard and skewered three men through the heart with it.

If you work in an office with Mr. T, **don't ask him for his three-hole punch.**

In the beginning there was nothing. And then Chuck Norris roundhouse kicked that nothing in the face and said, "Get a job." That is the story of the universe.

Coroners refer to dead people as "ABCs": Already Been Chucked.

When Mr. T goes to donate blood, he declines the syringe and instead requests a handgun and a bucket.

What was going through the minds of all of Chuck Norris's victims before they died? **His shoe.**

Mr. T destroyed the periodic table because he only recognizes the element of surprise.

Chuck Norris doesn't have a computer. Just a basement full of Asian kids who memorize numbers.

Late one night, while working hard on an academic paper about retrocausality, Mr. T inadvertantly invented the Manwich.

If you are within one mile of Chuck Norris and you drop your toast, it will always land butter-side up. Always.

Mr. T doesn't want your pity.

Chuck Norris doesn't believe in rubber condoms. Instead, he sticks his penis in a girl, and uses that girl as a condom while fucking another.

The French did not send the Statue of Liberty to the United States as a sign of peace. They were trying to win a bet that Chuck Norris couldn't fuck a one-hundred-fifty-foot-tall copper woman. Boy, were they wrong.

Mr. T's family wraps his holiday presents in lead so he can't see what's in them.

Chuck Norris invented the Spanish language because he liked the word *pantalones* and needed a language to use it in context.

Mr. T once punched Chuck Norris at the exact moment Chuck Norris roundhouse kicked Mr. T in the chest. The result was the '80s.

What happens when an irresistible force meets an immovable object?

Only Chuck Norris and Mr. T will ever know.

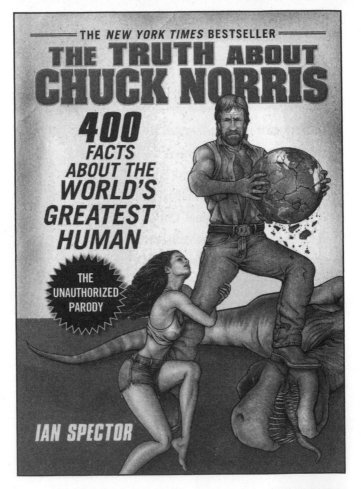

The first book to go behind the beard to reveal the real Chuck Norris

GOTHAM BOOKS a member of Penguin Group (USA) • www.penguin.com